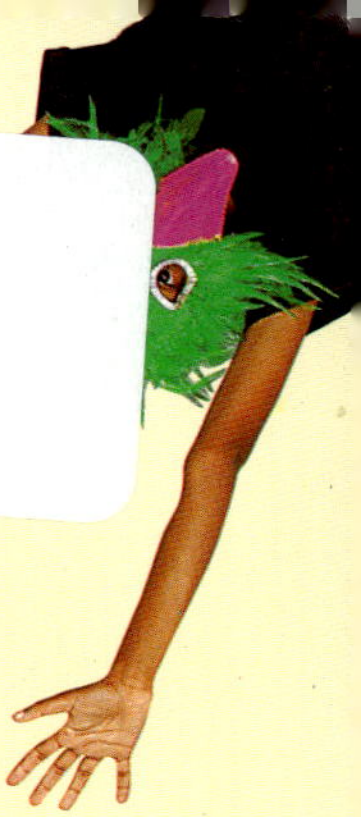

Magnificent Masks

Contents

A World of Masks

Written by Michele Paul

Masks are everywhere!
All over the world,
people wear masks.
They wear them
to tell stories.
They wear them
to hide who they are.
They wear them
to act like someone else.
They wear them just for fun!

This mask is from Brazil.

People from Mali make masks.
Some masks have hair on them.
Some masks have beads on them.
People use these masks for traditional dances.

In China, some people wear a mask at Chinese New Year to do the dragon dance. The dragon dance is an exciting part of Chinese New Year.
One person wears a big mask of the dragon's head.
Other people wear a costume for the dragon's body.
People watch as the dragon dances in the street.

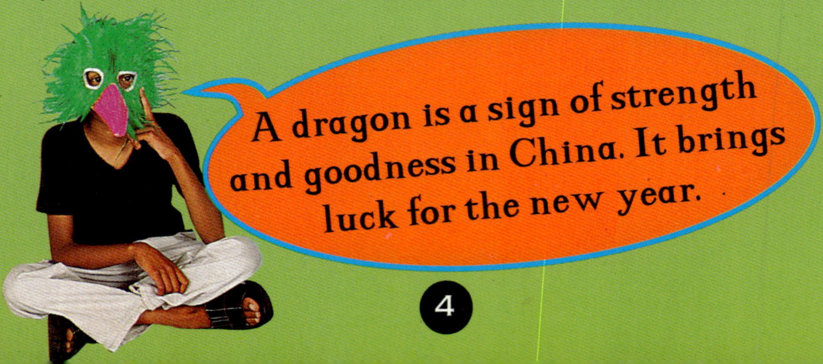

People from Puerto Rico
make masks out of papier-mâché
(*PAY per MAH shay*).
They use these masks for festivals.
The masks have horns and scary faces.
They are part monster and part animal.
They come from Spanish and African traditions.
They are thought to scare away bullies.

Inuit people from Alaska, Canada, and Greenland make masks for dancing and ceremonies.

Each mask has a special meaning. The masks are made out of wood and feathers. They are carved with metal tools.

Yuit people from Alaska
and Siberia make masks.
They make these masks
from caribou hide.
(Caribou is a kind of deer.)
These masks are for dancing.

People wear masks to festivals.
In New Orleans, people wear all sorts of masks for a big festival called Mardi Gras.
They wear the masks to hide who they are.
They wear them just for fun!

Sometimes actors use masks in plays,
on TV, or in movies.
They use them to make you laugh.
They use them to scare you.
Masks can make them look older.
Masks can make them look like monsters.
Masks can make them look like almost anything!

Eddie Murphy played all of these parts in the movie The Nutty Professor. He wore latex masks to change his face.

Master *of* Masks

An Interview with Jacob Rajan

Written by Kuljit Kaur

Jacob Rajan is a writer and an actor. He uses masks in his plays.

The first play Jacob wrote was called *Krishnan's Dairy.* It is about two people who work in a small shop.

Jacob as Gobi

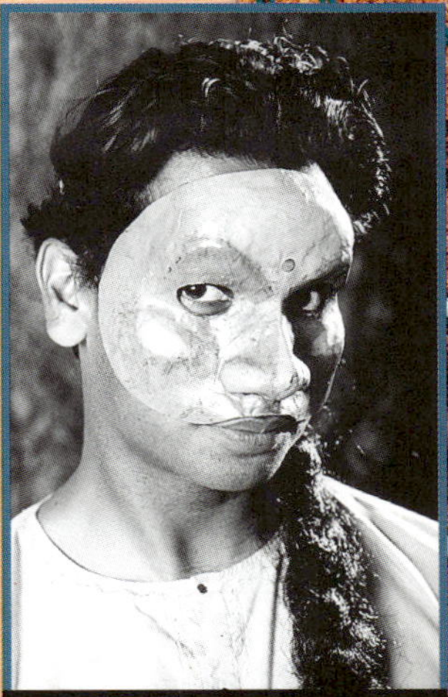
Jacob as Zina

There are two characters in the play. Jacob used masks to play both parts. He changed the masks very quickly.

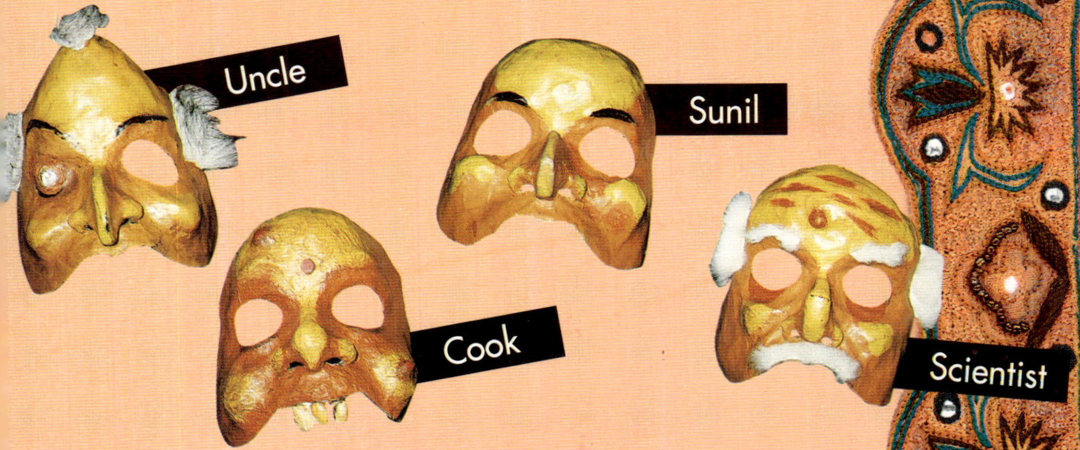

Three years later, Jacob wrote a play called *The Candlestick Maker.* There are four characters in the play. He played all of them, too!

Q. Why do you use masks in your plays?

A. People like masks in a one-person play. It helps them to believe in the characters.

Q. Who makes the masks?

A. My codirector, Justin Lewis, and I make the masks. We make them out of papier-mâché.

Q. How do you keep track of the masks?

A. I keep the masks in my pocket. There is only one mask in my pocket at one time. If I need three masks for one scene, then a person onstage will hold the other masks for me.

Q. Is it hard to change the masks?

A. I get used to it.
I wear a face mask that is held in place by elastic.
The other masks clip over it.

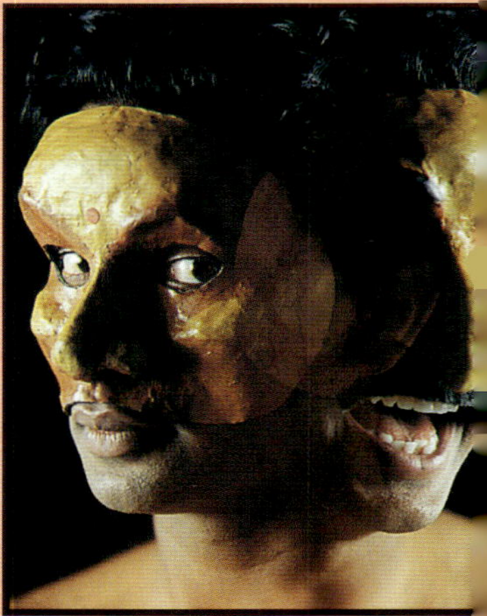

Jacob is wearing his face mask.
He is ready to clip his character mask on top.

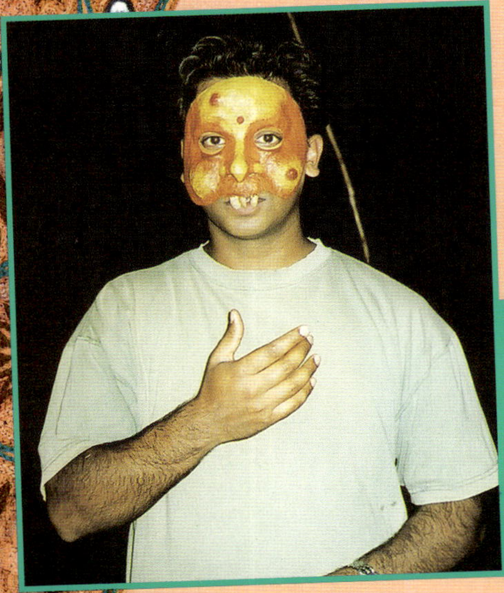

Jacob has clipped on his character mask. Onstage, Jacob turns away from the audience and changes his masks quickly.

Q. How much do you have to rehearse?

A. At first I have to rehearse a lot, but after a while I know what to do.

Q. Have you ever made a mistake?

A. Yes.
Once I put on
the wrong mask.
I said, "I am not feeling
like myself today."
People liked it
because it was funny.
It was a good way
to get around
the mistake.
That is the great thing
about a play.
Anything
can happen!

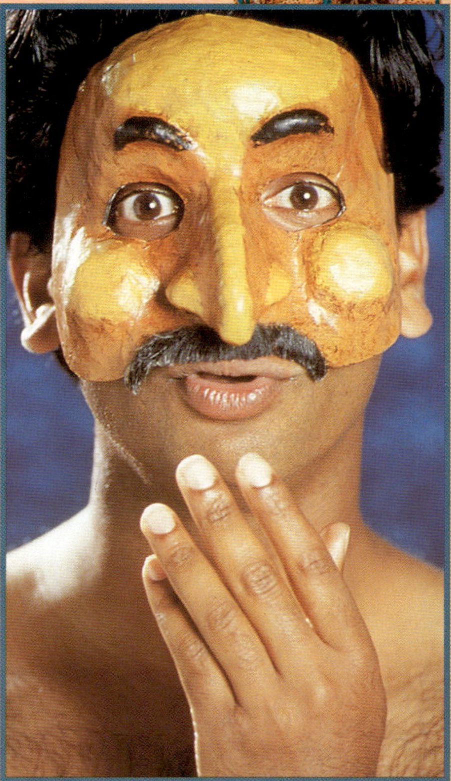

MAKING MASKS

Written by Victoria St John
Photographed by Glenn Jowitt

To make a papier-mâché rabbit mask, you will need:

Torn white paper

Paste

Glue

Toothpicks

Cardboard teeth

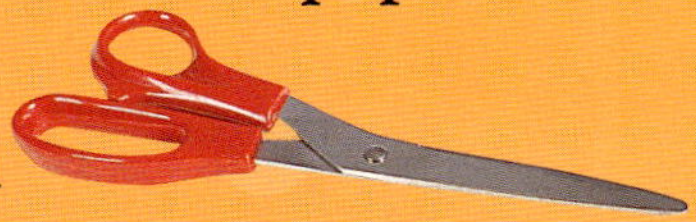
Scissors

Torn newspaper

Part of an egg carton

Elastic

Balloon

Paint and brush

Cardboard ears

Step 1

Paste torn newspaper all over the balloon. Make sure there are lots of layers of newspaper.

Step 2

Paste white paper over the newspaper. This makes it easier to paint later. Leave it to dry.

Step 3

When the paper is dry,
cut the end off the balloon.

Step 4

Cut the balloon to make a mask shape.
Cut out the eyeholes.

Step 5

Stick the toothpicks
in the egg carton to make whiskers.
Glue the teeth to the nose.

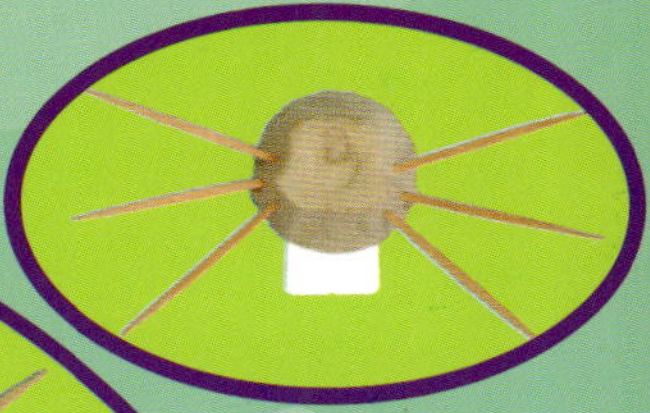

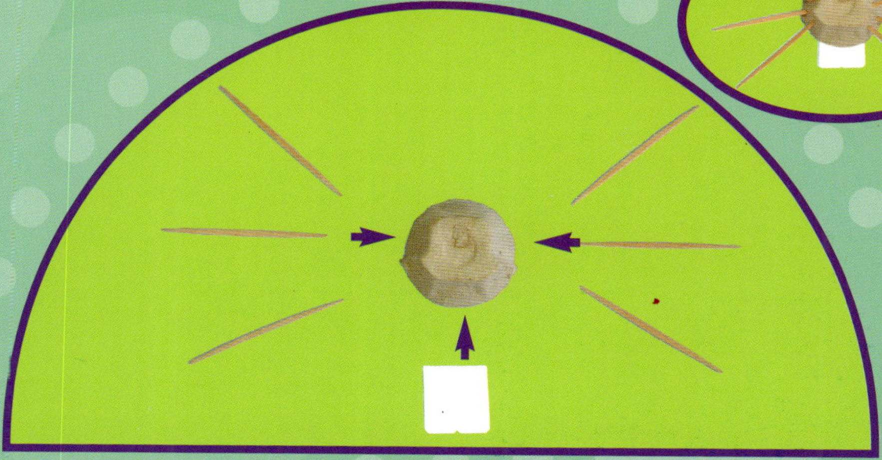

Step 6

Glue on the nose and ears.

Step 7

Paint the mask.

Step 8

Make small holes on the sides
of the mask and tie on some elastic.

Now have some fun with your mask.

You can also make masks for the animals in the play on page 22.

Rabbit's Revenge

A Play Based on a Traditional African Tale

Illustrated by Ben Archer

If you cannot find four people to perform this play, you can use the four different masks you have made to act all the parts yourself.

The Cast

Narrator

Rabbit

Elephant

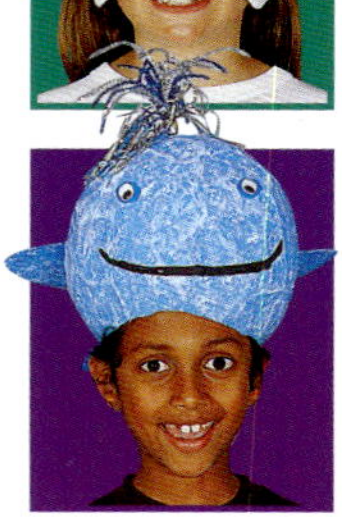

Whale

SCENE 1
Setting: The Jungle

Narrator

One day, Rabbit was making her way through the jungle. She saw Elephant.

Rabbit

Hello.
Fine day, isn't it?
Do you want to play a game?

Elephant

Go away, Rabbit.
I don't have any time for someone so little and weak.

Rabbit

Oh! How rude!

How would you feel if someone said this to you?

SCENE 2
Setting: The Seashore

Narrator

Rabbit was surprised
that Elephant talked
to her like that.
She went away to think about it.
Then she saw Whale out in the sea.

Rabbit

Whale! Please come here!
I would like to talk to you.

Narrator

Whale came over
to see who was talking to him.

Whale

Rabbit!
Did you just call me over here?

Rabbit

Yes, I did.

Whale

Who do you think you are?
You are too little and weak
to have anything to say to me.

Rabbit

Oh! How rude!

Narrator

Rabbit thought about
what Whale had said.
She felt hurt, but then she came up
with a plan.

Rabbit

Whale! You think I am weak,
but I am stronger than you.
You wouldn't be rude to me
if I beat you at tug-of-war.

Whale (laughing)

OK, Little One.
Go and get a rope,
and we will see who is stronger.

SCENE 3
Setting: The Jungle

Narrator

Rabbit went off to get
the strongest vine she could find.
On the way, she saw Elephant.

Rabbit

Elephant, you were rude to me.
I will have to show you
that I am stronger than you!

Elephant

How will you do that, Little One?

Rabbit

By beating you at tug-of-war.

Elephant (laughing)

All right.
I will play tug-of-war with you.

Rabbit

Good! Take this end of my vine.
Wait until I say ***pull***.
Then pull as hard as you can.

SCENE 4
Setting: The Seashore

Narrator

Rabbit took the other end
of the vine to Whale.
He took hold of it.

Rabbit

Now I've got the other end.
When I say ***pull***,
swim as fast as you can.

Whale

OK, Little One.

Rabbit (hiding behind a tree)

Pull!

(Elephant and Whale walk and
swim away, pulling on the vine.)

Elephant

My goodness!
Rabbit is much stronger
than I thought she would be.

Whale

That little Rabbit
could not be stronger than me!

(Elephant and Whale both strain
as they pull. The vine snaps.
They both fall offstage.
Rabbit walks off, laughing.)

Narrator

Elephant flew into the jungle
and hit a tree.
Whale flew through the sea
and hit a reef.

Elephant and Whale never did
figure out how little Rabbit had
beaten them, but they were
never rude to her again!

Index